W9-AVA-718

Behind the Wheel of a
CHOPPER

BY ALEX MONNIG

The Child's World
childsworld.com

Published by The Child's World®
1980 Lookout Drive • Mankato, MN 56003-1705
800-599-READ • www.childsworld.com

Acknowledgments
The Child's World®: Mary Berendes, Publishing Director
Red Line Editorial: Design, editorial direction, and production
Photographs ©: Shutterstock Images, cover, 1, 4, 8; iStockphoto, 7, 18; Jean-Yves Ruszniewski/TempSport/Corbis, 10; Mark Baker/AP Images, 12; Robert Mandel/iStockphoto, 14; Andrey Armyagov/Shutterstock Images, 16; Ed Kashi/VII/Corbis, 20

ISBN 9781634074278

LCCN 2015946340

Printed in the United States of America
Mankato, MN
December, 2015
PA02282

Table of
CONTENTS

Chapter 1

RIDING DANGEROUSLY

I t is a beautiful fall morning. The air is crisp but not too cold. There is a slight breeze. The sun is shining. It is a perfect day to be out riding a chopper.

You have planned to meet up with your friend to go for a ride. You wheel your bike out to the front of your house to wait for him. The chopper is shiny and clean. You washed it last night.

There is a bright-red number eight on the side of the bike. It stands out against the black finish of the rest of the bike.

Your chopper is a modified motorcycle. It is like a puzzle you put together. You made each piece just how you like it. It has a long front section with high silver handlebars. They gleam in the sunlight. Your bike's top speed is almost 100 miles per hour (161 km/h).

◄ **Choppers are personalized motorcycles.**

Your friend arrives at your house. He is not wearing his helmet. Helmets are an important part of motorcycle riding. It is against the law to ride without one in your state. But your friend does not always follow the rules.

Your friend is also the best rider you know. You decide to follow his example. You leave your helmet at home.

The two of you take off. The chopper hums nicely. You recently put in a new engine with your friend's help. You have spent a lot of time working on the bike. It feels good to ride it. You are going pretty fast. Houses and cars whiz by in a blur.

All of a sudden, a gray van ahead of you drifts into your lane. It is coming straight at you. And it is not slowing down. If you jam your brakes, you might skid out of control. The same thing could happen if you try to swerve out of the way too quickly. Worst of all, you are not wearing your helmet.

It is against the law in many states to ride a motorcycle ▶ without wearing a helmet.

Chapter 2

GETTING STARTED

You first learned about choppers from your dad. He taught you what he had learned from his dad—your grandpa. When you were little, your dad used to take you into the garage to show you your grandpa's choppers.

Choppers are motorcycles with a twist. They have two wheels and an engine like regular motorbikes. But your grandpa's choppers looked a lot different from other bikes.

This is because they were **custom** made. Every bike was different because all the parts were unique. Builders "chopped" up bikes. They removed unnecessary parts.

You got many of the ideas for your chopper from seeing other people's bikes. Many choppers have long, high handlebars that riders reach up to grab. They are slightly above shoulder height. Most standard motorcycle's handlebars sit just above the rider's waist.

◀ **People remove parts from choppers to make them look more simple.**

▲ **Many choppers have extended metal rods connecting the handlebars to the front tire.**

Chopper seats are different, too. Chopper riders sit in a reclined position farther away from the handlebars. Often the seats rise up in back to support the reclining riders.

Your grandpa was part of the early wave of chopper riders in the 1940s after World War II. He had been in Europe during the war. While over there, he and other soldiers had ridden lighter, faster motorcycles. And they liked the way the bikes felt.

Your dad told you that after the war, riders decided to chop up heavier American bikes. This made them more like the European bikes they had ridden in Europe. The chopper movement had begun.

As you got older, you became more interested in choppers. You loved seeing all the different parts your dad brought home. You looked forward to learning about new chopper parts. Sometimes, when it was safe, your dad let you help him install the parts on the bike.

AMERICAN CHOPPER

The TV show *American Chopper* helped make choppers more popular. The show started in 2002 and eventually expanded into multiple versions. It **showcased** the Orange County Choppers shop in New York. Customers would come to the shop to have their crazy chopper ideas brought to life. The show ran for ten years.

▲ The show *American Chopper* featured
custom-made choppers.

All of your dad's bikes were different. No chopper was
exactly the same. That is what drew you to building one. Tires,
handlebars, seats, and paint jobs were just a few of the things you
dreamed of customizing to make the perfect ride.

Finally, your dad told you that you were old enough to have
your own chopper. He bought you a motorcycle to mold into your
own bike. The first thing you did was strip off the old parts and
pieces. You and your dad then bought a new brown leather seat

with a tall back. He helped you measure where it should sit on the body of the chopper.

You also got some new silver handlebars. They rose up just above your shoulders. They looked a lot like the ones your dad had on his bikes. But yours bent in a way you had not seen anywhere. They had just the right shape.

Then came the best part. You had looked forward to choosing the look of the chopper's body. You wanted the look of your bike to have special meaning for you and your family.

Suddenly, an idea hit you. Your dad had seven choppers of his own. Yours would be your family's eighth.

With your dad's help, you spray-painted the body of the bike sky blue. Then you made a stencil. You used it to paint a red number eight on the body.

You came back a few hours later with your dad. The paint had dried. It looked perfect. It was time to practice riding.

Chapter 3

READY TO RIDE

It took a long time before you were ready to ride a chopper on your own. Your dad taught you the basics in your garage. He said the most important thing to remember was safety.

For protection, your dad handed you a shiny black helmet. He told you it was illegal in your state to ride without one. Next, he handed you a dusty old jacket and a pair of gloves. You already had on long pants and closed-toed shoes. Your dad said these things would help protect you in case you got in an accident.

All dressed, you took a step toward the chopper. You could not wait to start cruising around. But there was still more to learn. Even with the right equipment, it could be dangerous to drive a chopper, your dad told you. You had to follow the same rules as other drivers. You could not weave in and out of cars. You had to signal when you planned to change lanes. And you had to make

◄ Before stepping onto a chopper, riders must learn to be safe.

▲ Like brake pedals in cars, hand levers control choppers' brakes.

sure drivers could see you when they changed lanes. There was a lot to remember.

It took weeks to learn everything you needed to know about riding a chopper. Finally, you took a test to prove your knowledge. You passed with flying colors. Passing the test gave you permission to practice riding your chopper.

You started riding in a parking lot. Your dad walked next to the bike as you got used to balancing on it. You soon found out that balance was **critical** to riding. Too many sudden movements made you fall over. You did not want to think about what this would be like at a high speed.

Slowly but surely you started to get the hang of it. You felt comfortable leaning back in your seat with your arms stretched out in front of you. You learned how hard you needed to accelerate to get the bike up to speed and how sensitive the brakes were. You also got a feel for leaning from side to side to change direction.

Soon your dad took you out on the road. You started on quiet streets with few cars. You slowly started driving on busier streets. This helped you get used to riding around cars. Then it was time for your motorcycle **license** test. Your dad had trained you well. You passed on your first try. You were free to hit the highways.

Chapter 4

CLOSE CALL

On the road, the gray van continues to head toward you. You were ready to enjoy a day of riding with your friend. But now that is the furthest thing from your mind.

If you hit the brakes too hard, your wheels might lock up and send you skidding out of control, or you could flip over the front of your bike. If you lean too strongly to swerve out of the way, you might fall off your bike at a high speed.

You decide to tap your breaks to slow down, and you veer to the right. There are no other cars coming on the road. The gray van passes on your left. It is so close you can feel the breeze as it speeds by. Out of the corner of your eye you see the driver looking down at his cell phone. He has no idea how close he came to hitting you.

You pull over to the side of the road. Your friend pulls up alongside you. You are shaking.

◄ **Chopper riders should drive carefully to avoid accidents.**

▲ Motorcycle drivers should be careful to stay out of
car mirrors' blind spots.

He asks if you are okay. You are unhurt. But that was way too
close. The van could have hit you. You could have died.

Both you and your friend have learned your lesson. You were
lucky this time. You tell each other you will always wear a helmet

when riding. You even shake on it to seal the promise. You both start walking your choppers home.

You just had a near-death experience. But you smile as you look at the body of your chopper. The love of choppers had been passed down from your grandfather to your dad, and now it has been passed on to you.

A DANGEROUS HOBBY

Riding choppers and other motorcycles incorrectly can be deadly. In 2013, more than 4,300 riders were killed in accidents in the United States. That is an average of more than 11 every day. Many of these deaths are at least in part due to riders not wearing helmets. Head injury is the leading reason for death in motorcycle crashes.

GLOSSARY

critical (KRIT-i-kuhl): Critical things are very important and have a direct impact on an outcome. Balance is critical for riding a chopper.

custom (KUHS-tuhm): Something is custom when it is made specifically for a person. Custom choppers match their riders' tastes.

illegal (ih-LEE-guhl): Something is illegal when it is against the law. It is illegal in many states to ride a motorcycle without a helmet.

license (LAHY-suhns): A license is something a local government gives that allows people to do something. Riders need a special license to drive a chopper.

reclined (ri-KLINED): Somebody is reclined when he or she is leaning back. Chopper riders are slightly reclined when they ride.

showcased (SHOH-kaysd): Something is showcased when it is displayed for others to see. The Orange County Choppers shop was showcased on the *American Choppers* TV show.

stencil (STEN-suhl): A stencil is a piece of material with an outline of a shape or pattern cut out of it. Using a stencil can help a person paint more precisely.

TO LEARN MORE

Books

Dayton, Connor. *Choppers*. New York: PowerKids Press, 2007.

Lane, Billy. *Billy Lane's How to Build Old School Choppers, Bobbers and Customs*. Saint Paul, MN: MBI Publishing Company, 2005.

Mayes, Alan. *Old School Choppers*. Iola, WI: Kraus Publications, 2006.

Web Sites

Visit our Web site for links about choppers:
childsworld.com/links

Note to Parents, Teachers, and Librarians: We routinely verify our Web links to make sure they are safe and active sites. So encourage your readers to check them out!

SELECTED BIBLIOGRAPHY

Halsey III, Ashley. "U.S. Motorcycle Deaths Declined in 2013." *Washingtonpost.com*. The Washington Post, 6 May 2014. Web. 16 Jun. 2015.

Harley, Bryan. "History of Chopper Motorcycles." *MotorcycleUSA.com*. Motorcycle USA, 16 May 2009. Web. 16 Jun. 2015.

"History of Choppers." *Choppers.com*. Brand X Choppers, n.d. Web. Jun. 16, 2015.

INDEX

ABOUT THE AUTHOR

Alex Monnig is a freelance journalist from Saint Louis, Missouri, who now lives in Sydney, Australia. He graduated with his master's degree from the University of Missouri in 2010. During his career, he has spent time covering sporting events around the world.